I0472339

CONTENTS

WHY DO I NEED DIGITAL MARKETING?

In today's 24/7 economy, effective use of Digital Marketing gives your brand or business the potential to reach an audience of infinite size. Because the place in which your brand or business sits doesn't adhere to the old regime of 9 till 5 business hours, and because borders, both physical and otherwise are now irrelevant to business. It is more important than ever to ensure firstly that you have a digital marketing plan, secondly that it allows you to effectively target the correct audience, and last but certainly not least, being able to adapt to further growth and change, particularly in market size or trends. Digital Marketing brings with it the opportunity for businesses and brands alike, to easily view the metrics, allowing them to measure the engagement and success of their campaigns.

There are hundreds of free to use tools available on the internet that allow even the smallest of businesses or brands to view their engagement levels. Being a beginner at marketing metrics can be daunting! But we recommend that every business Multinational or run from your spare room invest time in engaging with online metric services. To put it plainly, businesses and brands that don't engage with social media, or with digital marketing risk potentially missing out on significant portions of their target market.

It's important to remember we are living and working in the 'Facebook Generation' and need to readily adapt to all that it offers. Don't just set up a Facebook page and think that's enough, invest time in understanding the tools available and how best you should utilise them.

CREATE A DIGITAL MARKETING PLAN

It is very rare to find that small business owners started their businesses, just because they love to do marketing. Don't get me wrong, the marketing industry is very interesting to work in, constantly evolving and creating opportunities to learn. But small business owners, want and need to be focusing on their passions, the reasons why they started their business. By producing a thorough marketing plan, small business owners allow themselves to plan ahead and be able to focus on what they love. An effective marketing plan will allow you identify and reach your target audience, grow your customer base and grow your sales.

Developing a plan forces you to think, formulate and articulate your thoughts regarding your customers, your product and how you can bring these two together. Too often Small to medium businesses settle for "selling more than last year" as their goal or metrics to judge their success. Measurable goals planned out through your marketing plan allows you to create tangible targets for you and your team to work towards.

An effective plan will help you organise your time and prioritise your goals. You only have so many hours in your day and only so many of those hours are able to be focused on marketing channels, being able to plan and schedule your marketing activities will allow you to work more efficiently during this time. There are hundreds of programs available online to allow small business owners to schedule and plan their digital marketing across numerous channels. Having a consistent Digital strategy will grow your brand recognition with potential consumers.

A marketing plan will allow you and your team to be on the same page, whilst ensuring consistency to your messaging. You as the business owner may undertake all the marketing activities, however it is essential for your staff to be aware of all promotions and activities. This allows them to present a professional face when communicating with both potential and current customers.

Marketing budgets are finite, deciding where your businesses priorities lie in advance will allow you to allocate your resources accordingly. Having a thought-out plan means when a new strategy or idea comes along you can know quickly whether it is worth pursuing. Your plan will allow you to be proactive and not reactive. Reactivity is a besetting problem for many small businesses, we often don't have the resources to anticipate everything in days or weeks in advance. Whilst this can sometimes be seen as a strength, because small business tends to be very flexible and are able to handle shifting conditions quickly, it also makes carrying out a disciplined course of action more difficult. Writing a plan gives your business the ability to know what your reaction to things ought to be in advance, which allows you to prepare your response when the market changes.

CREATE A BRAND IDENTITY

What do we classify as a brand identity? Is it your logo? Your Colour Palette? Your Infographic styles? Your font? It is all of that and so much more. Every brand in the market has an identity of its own depending on its offerings and the way of dealing with the customers, employees and stakeholders. A good brand identity will work wonders for your business and allow it to stand out from your competitors.

Before you start building out your brand identity elements, it is important to set out clear outlines for who you are as a business, what your product is, how you would like to be seen by your consumers and what you believe differentiates you to your competitors. If you use a professional design firm, they will ask for these details within their initial brief.

Depending on the size and classification of your business your brand identity needs change. Typically, all businesses need at very least a logo, Brand colours, typography, brand messaging i.e. Copy style.

A brands identity is a system of design, each individual element influences the next.

Starting with your logo, design can begin by simply sketching up ideas with pencils. As your design progresses it is important to find your core shapes and complementary imagery. At these early stages it is important that all designs must be in black and white, it is important that you ensure the core imagery is powerful enough to deliver the message on its own, without the enhancement of colour.

Once you have established your core visual imagery, it is time to explore colour. Colour may be something that you have already established within your company, you should still consider whether your current colours suit the desired imagery and messaging of your business. A professional colour palette is traditionally clean and flexible, this allows you to be creative in your messaging and imagery, giving you the option to mix up the colours if it becomes necessary. A flexible palette contains 1 main colour, 2 Primary colours, 3 – 5 complementary colours and 2 accent colours.

Typography is simply the set of fonts you choose to represent the brand on your website, graphics, signs and print materials. Typography should be informed by the shapes and core design pf your logo. Most would think this to be a simple choice, but typography is just as important to your branding as your logo, all must work in unison. It is important to limit the number of font families to 2-3. Generally, this sets out as a primary typeface for things such as headings, then secondary typeface's for specific circumstances such as tagline or body copy.

When it comes to brand messaging, we refer to the tone that the business uses when it communicates to consumers, whether that be through imagery or through copy (Text). It is essential that the tone of the businesses messaging is consistent with the rest of the brands identity, and that is kept with a consistent tone for all messaging on behalf of the brand i.e. if the brand identity specifies a fun, excited tone all copy should match that. The only acceptance to this rule is changing tone to match that of public sentiment.

PROFESSIONAL VISUAL CONTENT

The visual content on your social accounts or website play an important role in ensuring your customers stay engaged, as well as assist in moving them through the buying process. More often than not, your readers making the decision on whether or not they will continue to read or take any actions on your post with in the first few seconds. It is important that your visual content accurately shares your messaging, whilst being in line with your brand identity.

It is of absolute importance that all your visual content looks professional. I don't mean your post should be on a white back drop with Arial typeface much like I word document, I mean that it should look and feel Professional. Regardless of what your colour scheme is, if you are making your visual content on Word or Paint you are doing it wrong. We aren't all designers, but that doesn't mean we can't take advantage of Free or low-priced software online available to make your content.

Smart phones have allowed us all to have the ability to take quality photos and video with relative ease. My top tip to all budding small businesses is to set some time aside for a small photo shoot, this allows you to build up a bank of images that can be easily used for Digital content. If for instance, you are a tradesman who regularly moves between work sites. It is important that you take a small number of quality photos of your work following completion. The rule of thumb is that you should be as proud of your digital content as you are of your product.

Creating professional video content isn't as simple. However, the top 3 tips are to keep it simple, keep it 30 seconds or less, and finally to be mindful of what sound is attached, if in doubt remove or mute sound before posting. The biggest issue with video content is that often small businesses try to make it too elaborate, by adding effects or using abstract camera angles. It is important to note that if a viewer isn't comfortable and enjoying the viewing experience they will quickly scroll by. Facebook and Instagram use rather small metrics to measure views on videos, either 10 second views or 3 second views. Keeping videos short allow you to more accurately measure views and engagement with the content. Sound on videos is something many small businesses struggle with. They either include awkward small talk from the person shooting it, noise from third parties such as traffic or sound tracks that fit the video or setting. Simply it is better for a video to have no sound rather than the wrong sound. If you have the ability to choose the right soundtrack without infringing copy right then you should, if not leave it on mute.

WHAT IS SEO AND WHY IS IT SO IMPORTANT?

In a world built on Social media platforms, having your own website or base to direct traffic too, display large work portfolios, have an online storefront or a place to register potential leads. And this is why an effective SEO strategy will go a long way for your business.

Search Engine Optimization (SEO) refers to the method used to increase a website's position on search engine results pages (SERPs) on sites such as Google, Yahoo, or Bing. Developing an SEO strategy for your business can help draw consumer traffic to your website as well as grow your sales and revenue. To get you started on your SEO strategy development, here is a little background to understand how search engines, such as Google, use metrics to rank organic search website placements.

The goal of a search engine is to provide unbiased results that deliver information you are looking for as quickly and as accurately as possible. In order to do this, search engines are capable of identifying all relevant information online and ranking them in order of quality and relevance. There are hundreds of factors that are involved when search engines rank websites in an organic search.

The actions you take to optimize your site will have a direct effect on your SEO ranking. Components such as H1 tags, the words used in your website meta description, content and keyword density, permalinks, and backlinks are some of many things that you can leverage to boost your ranking.

Of course, we're not all web developers or SEO experts, and to assist with this highly complicated field Website hosting services such as word press offer Tools aka Plugins that will automate and assist with the application of your strategy. This is not a small task but ensuring that your business is seen one of the first pages of search engines will undoubtedly lead to more leads and sales.

SET UP GOOGLE BUSINESS

Setting up your Google business account is relatively simple, and if you are just getting started with local SEO a Google business listing a great place to focus your early efforts. When people search for a product or service near them, they're usually very close to purchase. As I'm sure many of you have experienced, when doing a near me or location-based search Google will offer up a list of local google business that match the search terms. This is why it is so important that the information regarding your business that google displays when customers conduct a search is accurate, complete and optimized as possible.

If Google has already generated a business listing for your company, the first step is to claim it which is a relatively simple process. If no listing has been generated, you will have to manually register and verify it with google. To do this you will need a google account.

Google my Business is a free and very effective way to gauge how much interest your business listing has received through the search engine. It also allows you measure how well your advertising strategy has been at growing your business. Once you have set up google business, you are able to start advertising through google ad words. Simply put google AdWords provide ads at the top of your search results depending on the search terms and history. This can be a very effective and efficient technique in building your SEO rankings.

REBRANDING

Businesses often face the need to rebrand, it can be the result of many different things, including company growth, new management, a bad reputation or just an outdated image. Whatever the reason is it is important that the new branding is something that customers will remember. Rebranding can understandably be a very daunting task for many brands. Particularly when elements of your brand portfolio have been with you since foundation. The thought of changing your company or brand's identity is a scary one, however it may be exactly what is needed to move your brand forward.

To stay competitive in any market it is important for your business to evolve and re-branding is part of this evolution. To help find the courage to assist in updating your logo or brand identity we recommend looking at Coca Cola, a company with more than 100 years of experience and who have rebranded many times to meet their market.

At the end of the day, it is important to remember your brand is an asset and that it should work for you. A rebrand is not something you should take lightly, after all a company who is constantly rebranding will struggle to build any brand recognition with consumers. But if you have weighed up the cost and you believe your brand needs a refresh for whatever reason it is important to embrace the change, and don't be scared of committing to your new brand. Building a lasting brand requires commitment to yourself, your company, its culture and your clients.

If you are brave enough to run a small business, you are brave enough to fully commit. Changing only half your branding and operating somewhere between, the old and the new will only confuse customers and ruin your brand reputation. No one wants to purchase from an unprofessional operation.

WHY INSTAGRAM FOR BUSINESS?

The majority of small businesses choose to delve into the world of social media, and often focus their paid advertising efforts through Facebooks boosted post system. Which isn't necessarily bad, however it tends to be very single minded. Facebook and its paid advertising system work's more effectively when combined with an active Instagram account.

For small Businesses, one of the first key objectives is to acquire both customers and gain exposure to potential customers, and Instagram is a great way to achieve this. Instagram is inexpensive and very easy to learn, allowing the user to craft stories and messaging to send out to a large audience. Instagram largely relies on visual content, whilst there is copy (text) associated with most posts, the key to Instagram is the visuals.

Having an appealing and engaging Instagram allows you to have greater reach on the platform with over 700 million monthly users. While not all followers will engage, it is an opportunity to let your products do the talking for you, visual content will allow your engagement levels to soar.

TARGETED FOLLOWING

Don't get me wrong, Instagram isn't as easy as creating nice pictures and raking in the engagement. It takes time, and sometimes financial investment to help accounts grow. Not all Small Businesses have the financial capability to invest in enough Instagram ads to grow their account, and our solution to this is something we call targeted following.

Targeted following is simply going to your competitors Instagram page, looking at their images and who has engaged with them and following those people. You do have to exercise caution using this technique, some very misinformed businesses pay services to build their followers and what happens is they receive thousands of followers from outside of their service area, often from countries on the other side of the world. To help exercise this caution I advise starting with community organisations that match your target market rather than a competitor business i.e. if starting an account for a local gym, I would look at pages such as local football teams whose followers are likely to be part of my target market and following them.

This is a very slow process, but if you are starting with a business with relatively low recognition in the community and very little to no budget, this is the technique for you.

Caution: Instagram only allow you to follow 250 people per hour, and if you try to follow a large number more than that in a day, they will suspend certain functionalities of your account. It is important to operate within the guidelines and be patient, followers take time to build.

THE POWER OF HASHTAGS

Choosing the right hashtag has the ability to lead your brand or company in the direction of building brand recognition. Brand recognition is one of the two main aspects of Brand Awareness.

Brand Awareness is a fundamental dimension of Brand equity, and often considered to be a prerequisite of the consumers buying decision. Brand awareness may also influence a consumer's risk assessment and confidence as part of their purchase decision, Familiarity with the brand and its characteristics allows the consumer to feel safe in their purchase and lead to return purchases. Brand Awareness through either of its facets whether it be Brand recognition or brand recall is extremely important for every business regardless of its size. You might say but I'm not selling anything, I just paint houses but in fact whether you realise it or not you are selling as the product.

Whether it's painting houses or selling books, positive brand awareness leads to return customers and more sales. Returning customers turn into loyal customers, and a well-recognised hashtag allows loyal customers to do a number of things. The two most important aspects are being able to connect with each other, and being able to share their purchases with their followings, and as a result advertise your products on your behalf.

Hash Tags also have the ability to help establish the brand culture. Culture is a big part of people's lives. It influences views, values, humour, hopes, loyalties, as well as worries and fears. This is why Brand culture is so essential, for businesses of all sizes. It has the ability to give the brand an identity that consumers can identify with, by doing this companies are able to use culture to build their brands and grow their market share. Whilst hashtags can be great for both brands and companies alike, I'll use can be detrimental to both your social media posts, and social media accounts.

It is of upmost importance that all brands and companies research ALL hashtags used on posts, whether they be used for just a single post or an entire campaign, the potential risk to a brands public perception is astronomical and there for we always insist on researching before use.

5 RULES OF HASH TAGS

We have compiled what we believe to be the top 5 essential rules when using Hashtags on Social media.

Rule number1! Using more hashtags decreases the amount of interactions it receives. Platforms such as Pinterest and Instagram are the exceptions to the rule. It is always important to adjust the number of Hashtags used for each Platform.

Rule number 2! Use local Hashtags to build community reach and awareness. This will assist in allowing your brand to become part of the community rather than an outsider. Always make sure to research local hashtags, to ensure they align with your brand message and work effectively.

Rule number 3! Always make sure product or brand hashtags to create conversation. Using product or brand hashtags allow you to reach the preferred target audience and build a personal connection with the branding.

Rule number 4! Using search tools to review related hashtags and their popularity, and the messaging associated with them. Allhashtag.com and Hashtagify.me are free tools available online that allow you to view and review related hashtags. It is important to ensure you research and understand the existing meanings and origins of them to ensure you avoid tarnishing your brand with offensive, controversial or demeaning messaging

Rule Number 5! Be Creative! Instagram and other social platforms are a place for creativity, being different to your competitors allows you to differentiate your branding. When you use a hashtag continuously it becomes synonymous with your brand and will highlight your posts to the people outside your following, while allowing new followers to use your hashtag to go back through your posts.

THE POWER OF INSTAGRAM STORIES

Instagram's millions of daily users love the feature, and it can be really effective. The average time spent by users on Instagram since the introduction of stories is 28 minutes, with over one-third of them watching Stories every day. Studies show that 20% of Stories posted by a business result in direct interaction with users.

Currently if you have over 10,000 followers on your Instagram account, you can unlock additional features. One of the most prominent of them is the ability to post links on a Story so users can go directly where you want them to go. Live Instagram Stories is a growing trend. This is mainly because consumers seem to be attracted to live streams. This means that you can live stream events, host Q&A sessions, etc.

There is generally less preparation involved in creating Stories, as you can post as much as you like without being intrusive because users can choose whether to watch them or not. An added bonus is that as the post will disappear after 24 hours, you don't have to worry about making it quite so polished.

CROSS POSTING

Cross-posting on social media platforms is like putting text through Google Translate. You run the risk of getting a very weird result that looks careless and unintentional. Instead, your content should be fluent in the language of each platform. Otherwise you'll never be able to have a real conversation with your followers. Things like caption length, image formatting, and vocabulary differ by platform. Sharing the exact same post on all of them means you might accidentally end up inviting your followers to retweet you on Facebook or Pin your post on Instagram.

Speaking of your followers, they're not going to be the same on every platform. What they expect and like regarding your brand will differ between platform i.e. Instagram users may enjoy seeing stories regarding the behind the scenes operation of your business such as manufacturing, whereas the same story on Facebook may receive little to no engagement. You should still be posting regularly across all your social media accounts and engaging with your followers on each platform. But instead of repeating messages word-for-word, you should be writing a new post each time.

The new post doesn't need to be largely different, should still carry the same desired message. What should change is the intricacies of the posts that each individual platform uses.
Crafting unique messages might sound like a lot of work, but you don't need to start from scratch every time. Even small tweaks make a difference and show that you're paying attention. They're numerous online services that allow you to schedule your posts across numerous channels all well ahead of time. These tools make it viable to tweak the messages across platforms without having to go to each individual website.

WHERE TO NOW?

Do you feel ready to tackle the world of Digital Marketing?

If you said yes! Get into it! Start small and simple, explore every-thing available to you through social media, and then slowly but steady expand and connect to your audience through other plat-forms.

If you said No, you should do one of two things. You Should either spend some more time on social media, become comfortable in yourself, your abilities and whats available to you. Your second option, contact Fineapple for direction. we will try to direct you in the right direction and get you set up for success. To contact us head to www.fineapplemedia.com.

Subscribe to our mailing list, and follow our socials for a continu-ous stream of Digital Marketing updates, and skills that you can use to better your small business.

if you have any questions or enquiries please contact the team through our website. www.Fineapplemedia.com

Yours in Marketing,

Team FineApple.